# THE BOOK OF KERRYMAN JOKES

by

**DES MacHALE**

MERCIER PRESS

**MERCIER PRESS**
P.O. Box 5, 5 French Church St., Cork
16 Hume St., Dublin 2


Twentieth Edition, 1995
ISBN 0 85342 466 7

*This book is dedicated to Kerrymen everywhere.*

Typeset in 11point ITC Bookman by
Seton Graphics Ltd., Bantry, Co. Cork.

*Printed in Ireland by Litho Press Co., Midleton, Co. Cork.*

## INTRODUCTION

There is only one possible explanation for the spate of Kerryman jokes that has engulfed Ireland like a tidal wave for the last fifteen years or so — jealousy. After all, Kerry has won the All-Ireland football title more often than any other county; it has the Lakes of Killarney, held by many to have the most beautiful scenery in the world; and it has the Rose of Tralee competition, featuring the loveliest and most charming girls one can imagine. In addition, recent historical and religious research by John B. Keane seems to suggest that even the Holy Ghost was a Kerryman.

In the face of all this, the only feeble comeback that the rest of us can manage is the Kerryman joke — a pathetic attempt to preserve our self-esteem by promulgating the fallacy that Kerrymen are not quite as gifted intellectually as others. Even here we lose out, because some of the best Kerryman jokes are manufactured by Kerrymen who have acquired the ability to laugh at themselves, and this is surely the essence of a sense of humour, by any definition.

Nearly every country pokes fun at the inhabitants of one of its regions, or at the inhabitants of a nearby country. The English laugh at the Irish; the Europeans laugh at the Poles; and the Canadians laugh at the Newfoundlanders. But the Kerryman joke is never a straightforward insult. Any stupidity involved is always creative and more often than not has a touch of sheer genius about it. Historically, the Kerryman joke possibly has its origins in the Irish Bull, that unique blend of paradox and contradiction frequently found in Ireland.

It goes without saying that all Kerrymen in this book are purely ficticious, and any resemblance between them and any Kerryman, living or dead, is entirely coincidental. In actual fact Kerrymen are widely known for their wit, intelligence, and deviousness. As Ireland's principal storyteller and creator of tall stories, Eamon Kelly, himself a Kerryman, has said, 'You'd ate a bag of salt before you'd get to know a Kerryman.'

Kerryman jokes seem to be most popular in the cities of Dublin and

Cork. It is hardly a coincidence that many of the top jobs in these cities are held by Kerrymen. Need we look any further for a reason for the popularity of Kerryman jokes?

Have you heard about the Kerryman who got a pair of water skis for Christmas?

He's still going around looking for a lake with a slope.

* * *

A Kerryman had bought his first mirror and was using it while shaving. The mirror fell on the floor but fortunately was undamaged. As he gazed down at his face in the mirror he reflected: —

'Just my luck. I've only just bought a new mirror and I've gone and cut my head off.'

* * *

How do you recognise a Kerryman on an oil rig?

He's the one throwing crusts of bread to the helicopters.

* * *

A hotel manager noticed that one of his guests had signed himself XX in the register. He called round to the guest's room and found himself face to face with a Kerryman who explained, 'The first X stands for John O'Sullivan and the second X stands for M.A.'

* * *

Have you heard about the Kerryman who cheated Irish Rail? He bought a return ticket to Dublin and didn't go back.

* * *

A Kerryman attended a concert where a ventriloquist who fancied himself as a comedian told about twenty Kerryman jokes in a row.

'Look,' shouted the Kerryman, standing up in the audience, 'I'm fed up being insulted by all these jokes. We're not as stupid as you make out.'

'Please sit down sir and be calm,' said the ventriloquist, 'after all it's only a joke, and don't tell me that Kerrymen haven't got a sense of humour.'

'I'm not talking to you,' said the Kerryman, 'I'm talking to the little fellow on your knee.'

* * *

How do Kerrymen forge 10p pieces?
They cut the corners off 50p pieces!

* * *

A man hired a Kerryman as an assistant to take phone calls. One day the phone rang and when the Kerryman answered he hung up immediately.

'Who was that?' asked his boss.

'Some fool saying it was a long distance from New York. I told him everybody knew that.'

* * *

Two Kerrymen were sent to jail, one for thirty years and the other for thirty-five years. They happened to share the same cell, so on their first night in jail the Kerryman who got the longer sentence said to his cell-mate. 'You take the bed nearest the door, since you'll be released first.'

* * *

A Kerryman rang Aer Lingus and asked how long it took to fly from Dublin to London.

'Just a minute sir,' said the girl on the desk.

'Thank you,' said the Kerryman and hung up.

* * *

KERRY FOREMAN on a building site: 'How many men are working in that pit?'
VOICE FROM PIT: 'Three.'
KERRY FOREMAN: 'Well half of ye come up.'

* * *

A Kerryman got a job reading gas meters and after his first day's work arrived up at the pub with his pockets bulging with coins and ordered drinks for everybody.

'You seem to be in the money,' said the barman; 'I suppose it will be drinks all round again when you get paid at the weekend.'

'What,' said the Kerryman, 'do I get paid as well?'

* * *

Have you heard about the two Kerrymen who hi-jacked a submarine? They demanded half a million pounds ransom and two parachutes.

* * *

Have you heard about the Kerryman who damaged his health by drinking milk?
The cow fell on him.

* * *

A fellow walked into a bar in Dublin and asked the barman if he had heard the latest Kerryman joke,

'I'm warning you,' said the barman, 'I'm a Kerryman myself.'

'That's alright,' said the fellow, 'I'll tell it slowly.'

* * *

Have you ever seen a Kerryman's alarm clock?

It has a long piece of string attached. All he has got to do is pull the string five minutes before the time the clock is set for, and it wakes him.

* * *

'I'll never be able to understand,' said a Kerryman reading a newspaper, 'how people always seem to die in alphabetical order.'

* * *

How would you get a Kerryman to climb onto the roof of a pub?
Tell him the drinks are on the house.

* * *

Have you heard about the Kerryman who fed and starved his pigs on alternate days?
He wanted to sell them for streaky bacon.

* * *

Two Kerrymen emigrated to America, and were sitting in New York harbour thinking of home. A diver suddenly emerged from the water near where they sat.

'Will you look at that,' said one Kerryman to the other, 'why didn't we save the boat fare by walking to America?'

* * *

A Corkman was brought to court for pushing a Kerryman off the top of Cork's County Hall — the tallest building in Ireland.

'You shouldn't have done that you know,' said the judge, 'you might have hurt somebody walking below.'

* * *

A Kerrywoman out shopping met the doctor who was treating her husband.

'Did you take his temperature this morning as I told you?' he asked.

'Indeed I did doctor,' she replied, 'I took the barometer from the hall and put it on his chest. It said VERY DRY, so I gave him two bottles of stout and he recovered immediately.'

* * *

A Kerryman won a round-the-world cruise in a raffle. He refused to accept his prize because he said that he had no way of getting back.

* * *

A Kerry guard was giving evidence at a court case arising out of a motor accident.
'I measured the distance between the skid marks and the footpath,' he said, 'and found that it was exactly the same as the distance between the footpath and the skid marks.'

* * *

How do you keep a Kerryman happy for an afternoon?
Write P.T.O. on both sides of a piece of paper.

* * *

A Kerryman decided to become a terrorist and was assigned to hi-jack an aircraft. He didn't get on very well however. He planted a bomb in the plane and gave the pilot five minutes to leave the cabin.

* * *

*Announcement at a Dublin railway station:*

The next train for Galway will leave at 13.50 hours.

The next train for Wexford will leave at 14.25 hours.

The next train for Kerry will leave when the big hand is at the twelve and the little hand is at the four.

* * *

Two Kerrymen went to Maggie Thatcher and offered to dig the Channel Tunnel for £500.

'How do you plan to do it?' asked Thatcher.

'Well,' said one Kerryman, 'to speed up operations, I'll start to dig on the French side, while my colleague here will start to dig on the English side.'

'But,' protested Thatcher, 'what happens if there is even a slight error in your calculations, and you fail to meet?'

'Then,' said the Kerryman, 'you get two Channel Tunnels for the price of one.'

* * *

Why do Kerry dogs have flat faces?
From chasing parked cars.

* * *

How do you confuse a Kerryman?
Place three shovels against the wall, and tell him to take his pick.

* * *

A Kerryman was charged with murder and was sent for trial by jury.

To everyone's surprise he pleaded guilty. Nevertheless the jury returned a verdict of 'not guilty'.

'How on earth have you reached a verdict like that?' asked the judge, 'the man pleaded guilty.'

'You don't know him like we do, your honour,' said the foreman of the jury. 'He's the biggest liar in the country and you can't believe a word out of his mouth.'

* * *

An American tourist was boasting to a Kerryman about the fact that the Americans had just put a man on the moon.

'That's nothing,' said the Kerryman, 'we have plans to land a man on the sun.'

'That's crazy,' said the American, 'he would burn to a cinder before he got within a million miles of the sun.'

'We've thought of that too,' said the Kerryman, 'we're sending him at night.'

* * *

A fellow was charged with murder, so he bribed a Kerryman on the jury to have the jury find him guilty of manslaughter. After being out ten hours, the jury returned a verdict of manslaughter.

'I'll be for ever in your debt,' the defendant said to the Kerryman, 'how did you manage it at all?'

'I had a terrible job,' said the Kerryman, 'the other eleven wanted to acquit you.'

* * *

Have you heard about the Kerryman whose library was burned down?
Both books were destroyed, and worse still, one hadn't even been coloured in.

* * *

Two Kerrymen were working on a building site when one of them fell fifty feet from the scaffolding.

'Are you dead?' asked the first Kerryman.

'Yes,' replied the second.

'You're such a liar, I don't know whether to believe you or not,' said the first.

'That proves I'm dead, because if I was alive you'd never have the nerve to call me a liar,' said the second.

* * *

How many Kerrymen does it take to milk a cow?
Twenty-four. One to hold each teat, and twenty to lift the cow up and down.

* * *

A Kerryman bought a new car on a fantastic hire purchase scheme — 100% down and nothing to pay each month.

* * *

A Kerryman, who had fallen into a lot of money, went to the doctor with an injured leg.

'That looks nasty,' said the doctor, 'I'd better give you a local anaesthetic.'

'Hang the expense,' said the Kerryman, 'I'll have the imported one.'

* * *

A Kerryman had a mule whose ears were so long that every time he put him into the stable the mule grazed his ears on the top of the doorway. So the Kerryman decided to knock six inches off the wall over the doorway.

'Why don't you take away the ledge under the door?' asked a friend. 'It would be less dangerous and much less expensive.'

'Look,' said the Kerryman. 'it's the mule's ears that are causing the trouble, not his feet.'

* * *

Two Santa Clauses are outside a big store. Which one is the Kerryman?
The one with the bag of Easter eggs.

* * *

A Kerryman bought a large engagement ring for his girlfriend.

'Ooh,' she gasped, 'is it a real diamond?'

'If it's not,' said the Kerryman, 'I've just been done out of £1.50.'

* * *

What are Kerry nurses famous for?
Waking patients up to take their sleeping tablets.

* * *

Have you heard about the expedition of Kerrymen who set out to climb Mount Everest?
They ran out of scaffolding thirty feet from the top.

* * *

Have you heard about the Kerryman who thought that VAT 69 was the Pope's telephone number?

* * *

Have you heard about the Kerryman who lost all his luggage at Crewe Station?
The cork came out.

* * *

Did you hear about the Kerryman who saw a notice reading: — 'Man Wanted For Robbery and Murder'?
He went in and applied for the job.

* * *

How can a 4ft. 11 ins. Kerryman join the guards?
Only if he lies about his height.

* * *

Have you heard about the Kerryman who went to a drive-in movie?
He didn't like the show so he slashed the seats.

* * *

A Kerryman visited Harley Street and got an appointment with a famous plastic surgeon.

'Are you the famous plastic surgeon?' asked the Kerryman.

'I am that,' replied the plastic surgeon.

'In that case,' said the Kerryman, 'how much would it cost to have this plastic bucket mended?'

* * *

One Kerryman bet another that he couldn't carry him across Niagara Falls on a tightrope. After a hair-raising trip they made it to the other side. As one Kerryman handed over the bet of £100 to the other he sighed, 'I was sure I had won the bet when you wobbled halfway over.'

* * *

Then there was the Kerryman who joined the 75th regiment of the army, to be near his brother who was in the 76th regiment.

* * *

As the *Titanic* was sinking, a Kerryman was swimming madly round the ship, shouting, 'Where's the dance, where's the dance?'

'What do you mean, "dance"?' asked a drowning passenger.

'I heard an announcement only ten minutes ago,' said the Kerryman, 'a-band-on ship, a-band-on ship.'

* * *

A tailor's iron is called a 'goose'. A Kerry tailor wanted to buy two new irons, so he wrote away to the manufacturers as follows: —

Dear Sir,

Please send me two gooses. . .

After reading the letter he decided that this wouldn't do, so he changed it to

Dear Sir,

Please send me two geese. . .

However, he again felt that there was something wrong and that the manufacturers would be laughing at him. Finally he hit upon the following:

Dear Sir,

Please send me a goose. . .

P.S. While you're at it, you may as well send me a second one.

* * *

A Kerryman who went to London was shown great kindness by a Pakistani bus conductor. As he stepped off the bus, he said, 'Thank you very much sir, and I hope your head gets better soon.'

* * *

A lady hired a Kerryman to look after her goldfish. One day she asked him if he had changed the water in the goldfish bowl.
'Indeed I haven't,' he replied, 'they didn't drink what I gave them last week.'

* * *

A Kerryman who fell a hundred feet from a building was asked if the fall had hurt him.

'It wasn't the fall at all,' he replied, 'but the sudden stop.'

'I suppose,' he added after a few minutes' reflection, 'that I was lucky that the ground broke my fall.'

* * *

A Kerryman stated in his will that he wished to be buried at sea.
Three of his friends were drowned, digging the grave.

* * *

A Kerryman went to the doctor and complained that every time he drank a cup of tea he got a sharp pain in his eye.

'Have you tried taking the spoon out of the cup?' asked the doctor.

* * *

A Kerryman's brother died, so he decided he would put a death notice in the paper.

'How much does a death notice cost?' he asked the girl at the counter.

'£10 an inch,' she replied.

'I'll never manage to pay,' said the Kerryman, 'my brother was six foot four inches tall.'

* * *

A fellow played the following trick on a Kerryman.

'Listen,' he said, 'punch me on the hand as hard as you like,' placing his hand up against a brick wall.

The Kerrryman swung his fist but at the last moment the fellow pulled away his hand, and the Kerryman's fist went crashing into the brick wall.

After a good laugh, the Kerryman decided to try out the trick on his friend.

'Listen,' he said, 'punch me on the hand as hard as you like.'

He looked around for a wall but he couldn't find one.

'We would really need a brick wall to do this trick properly, but never mind, I'll hold my hand in front of my face.'

* * *

Why do you never get ice in drinks served in Kerry?
The fellow with the recipe emigrated.

* * *

A Kerryman was digging a hole in the ground, when a passer-by asked where he was going to put all the clay out of the hole.

'I'll dig another hole,' said the Kerryman.

'But how do you know it will all fit?'

'I'll dig the other hole deeper,' said the Kerryman.

* * *

How do you make a Kerryman laugh on a Monday morning?
Tell him a joke on Friday evening.

* * *

A Kerryman was attacked by a robber and put up a spirited fight before parting with his purse which contained only 15p.

'You mean to tell me you put up all that struggle, all for 15p?'

'No,' said the Kerryman, 'I thought you were after the £50 I've got hidden in my left shoe.'

* * *

What do you call a Kerryman on a bicycle?
A dope peddler.

* * *

A Kerryman applied for a job as an RTE newscaster, but was turned down. 'I'll bet I didn't get the job,' he complained, 'just because I'm a K-K-K-K-Kerryman.'

* * *

What has an I.Q of 144?
A gross of Kerrymen.

* * *

A Kerryman nearly became a hero by diving fully clothed into a river to rescue a drowning man. He only made one mistake — he hung the man up to dry on a tree by the river.

* * *

A Kerryman joined the army, but forgot to take his overcoat with him. His mother posted the coat to him, with the following note:

> Dear Son,
> I'm sending on your overcoat which you forgot. To save postage I've cut off the buttons.
> Your loving Mother.
> P.S. You'll find the buttons in the pocket.

* * *

How do you get £20 from a Kerryman? Ask him to lend you £40. Then say, 'Look give me £20. Then you'll owe me £20 and I'll owe you £20 and we'll be all square.'

* * *

A Kerryman's house caught fire, so he rushed to the nearest telephone kiosk and dialled very quickly.

'Hello, is that 999?'

'No, This is 998.'

'Well, would you nip in next door and tell them my house is on fire?'

* * *

A *Kerryman's definition of a negro:* A man so black that charcoal would leave a white mark on him.

* * *

Two Kerrymen were building a house.

'Hey,' said the first Kerryman, 'these nails are defective. The heads are on the wrong end.'

'You fool,' said the second Kerryman, 'those are for the other side of the house.'

* * *

A Kerryman who went to London had never seen traffic lights before, so he asked a policeman what they were.

'When the lights are red,' said the policeman, 'Englishmen are allowed to proceed, and when they are green Irishmen are allowed to proceed.'

'This a great country,' said the Kerryman, 'the Orangemen never get a chance.'

* * *

What do you call a Kerryman who marries a gorilla?
A social climber.

* * *

An American in a pub bet a Kerryman £50 that he couldn't drink ten pints of stout in ten minutes.

'You're on,' said the Kerryman, 'give me a few minutes to prepare myself,' and he vanished out the door. Fifteen minutes later he returned and drank the ten pints of stout in ten minutes.

'I knew I could manage it,' said the Kerryman, 'because I just did it in the pub next door.'

* * *

How do you brainwash a Kerryman? Fill his wellingtons with water.

* * *

Having visited all the animals in the Zoo, a Kerryman spent half an hour looking for the Exit, but finally decided that it must have escaped.

* * *

A Kerryman got a job as a deep-sea diver. One day he got the following message: —

'Come up immediately, we're sinking.'

* * *

An English tourist travelling around Kerry was horrified to see a cart loaded with hay, with two Kerrymen sitting on top, suddenly emerging into the narrow road from a field. He jammed on his brakes, but he couldn't stop in time, so in desperation he drove the car over the roadside hedge and into the field, where it burst into flames.

'Bejabers,' said one Kerryman to the other, 'some of these tourists are terrible drivers. We only just got out of that field in time.'

* * *

A Kerrywoman went to the Zoo and saw a notice over the Kangaroo's cage:

'A NATIVE OF AUSTRALIA'.

She turned to her friend, and said, 'And to think my sister married one of them things.'

* * *

Then there was the Kerryman who learned to cut his fingernails with his left hand, in case he ever lost his right.

* * *

*Some verdicts of Kerry juries:* —

(i) We find the man who stole the horse, not guilty.

(ii) not guilty, but we recommend that he doesn't do it again.

(iii) Unanimous — nine to three.

(iv) Your honour, we are all of one mind — insane.

(v) We return a verdict of guilty against the unknown attacker who murdered O'Shea.

* * *

Have you heard about the Kerryman who won the Nobel Prize for Agriculture? He was simply a man out standing in his own field.

* * *

Two Kerrywomen were talking at a bus stop:

'I don't know what to buy my little boy for his birthday,' said the first.

'Why not buy him a book?' asked the second.

'Don't be crazy,' said the first, 'he's got a book already.'

* * *

A little Kerry lad asked his mother if he could go outside to watch the eclipse of the sun.

'Yes,' she replied, 'but don't stand too near.'

* * *

A Kerryman was on the boat to Holyhead when there was a shout of 'Man overboard'. The Captain shouted 'throw in a buoy', so the Kerryman grabbed a little eight-year-old boy and threw him into the water.

'No, you fool,' said the Captain, 'I meant a cork buoy.'

'How the heck was I to know what part of Ireland he was from?' roared the Kerryman.

* * *

A Kerryman visiting the Zoo stood in front of the snake-house, putting his tongue out at the snakes.

'What's going on here?' asked a keeper.

'Look,' said the Kerryman, 'they started it.'

* * *

Kerry sergeant to his regiment during a battle: 'Keep firing men, and don't let the enemy know we are out of ammunition.'

* * *

A Kerryman, a Corkman, and a Clareman were in a queue to buy potatoes outside a grocer's shop.

'Sorry,' said the grocer, 'I'm not serving Corkmen today.' So the Corkman left the queue.

After a while the grocer reappeared and said, 'Sorry, I'm not serving any Claremen today.' So the Clareman departed.

Finally the grocer said 'Sorry, I have no potatoes at all today.' So the Kerryman said, 'That's just typical, serving the Corkman first.'

* * *

A fellow was explaining to a Kerryman how nature sometimes compensates for a person's deficiencies.

'For example,' he told him, 'if a man is deaf, he may have keener sight, and if a man is blind, he may have a very keen sense of smell.'

'I think I see what you mean,' said the Kerryman, 'I've often noticed that if a man has one short leg, then the other one is always a little bit longer.'

* * *

A Kerryman rushed into an insurance office and said, 'I'd like to buy some house insurance please.'

'Certainly sir,' said the clerk, 'just fill in these forms.'

'I can't wait that long,' said the Kerryman, 'my house is on fire.'

* * *

A Kerryman arrived up in Dublin and stood looking up at Liberty Hall. A Dubliner arrived on the scene and said, 'Look, you've got to pay me £1 for every storey of Liberty Hall you look up at. How many storeys did you look at?'

'Five,' said the Kerryman, and handed over £5.

'I certainly fooled him,' said the Kerryman to himself afterwards, 'I really looked at ten storeys.'

* * *

During the Emergency a Kerry regiment was sent to immobilise a railway station. After about five minutes they returned without a single casualty, and carrying a large sack.

'How did you manage to do it so quickly?' asked the Commander.

'Easy,' answered the regiment leader. 'We simply stole all the railway tickets.'

* * *

A Kerryman went to insure his car and paid £200 to have it insured against fire.

'For £100 more sir,' said the agent, 'you can insure it against theft also.'

'That would be a waste of money,' said the Kerryman, 'who would ever steal a burning car?'

* * *

How many Kerrymen does it take to launch a ship?
A thousand and one — one to hold the bottle of champagne, and a thousand to bang the ship against it.

* * *

Then there was the Kerryman whose wife had twins.
He went out with a shotgun looking for the other man.

* * *

What do you call a Kerryman under a wheelbarrow?
A mechanic.

* * *

Have you heard about the Kerryman who drove his new car over the cliff?
He wanted to test the air-brakes.

* * *

What do you do if a Kerryman throws a pin at you?
Run like mad — he's probably got a grenade between his teeth.

* * *

How do you recognise a Kerry pirate?
He's got a patch over each eye.

* * *

It's easy to recognise a firing squad consisting entirely of Kerrymen.

They stand in a circle so as to be sure of not missing. It's easy to tell if the prisoner is a Kerryman too.

If he is, he doesn't duck.

* * *

Have you heard about the Kerryman who had a brain transplant?
The brain rejected him.

* * *

Two Kerrymen lost on a dark night came upon a milestone.

'We must have wandered into a graveyard,' said the first.

'Some fellow called "Miles from Dublin" is buried in this grave,' said the second.

'You're right,' said the first, 'and look at the age he was — a hundred and seventy-five.'

* * *

A Kerryman went into a store and asked for four dozen mothballs.

'But,' said the shop assistant, 'you bought four dozen mothballs only yesterday.'

'That's right,' said the Kerryman, 'but those damn moths are very hard to hit.'

* * *

A Kerryman went to London and found himself in the Underground late one night. Seeing a notice DOGS MUST BE CARRIED ON THE ESCALATOR, he moaned to himself, 'Where am I going to find a dog at this hour of the night?'

* * *

A Kerryman went to the cinema and, having bought his ticket, went in to see the film. A few minutes later he came back to the box office and bought another ticket. Five minutes later he returned and bought a third ticket.

'Look,' said the girl a the ticket office, 'what are you playing at? That's the third ticket you've bought.'

'I know,' said the Kerryman, 'but there's a crazy guy inside who keeps tearing them up.'

* * *

A Kerryman was suffering from pains in his knees, so he visited the doctor.

'You're suffering from a disease that we medical experts call "kneeitis",' said the doctor. 'Take it easy for a month or so and above all don't climb any stairs. That puts a terrible strain on the knees.'

A month later the Kerryman returned and after a brief examination was found to have recovered completely.

'Can I climb the stairs now doctor?'

'Certainly,' replied the doctor.

'Thank Heavens,' said the Kerryman, 'I was getting a bit browned off climbing up the drainpipe every time I wanted to go to the toilet.'

* * *

How do you recognise the bride at a Kerry wedding?
She's the one wearing the white wellingtons.

* * *

A Kerryman who kept all his money in a mattress was asked why he didn't keep it in the bank, in view of all the interest he would receive.

'I've thought of that too,' said the Kerryman, 'I put a little away every week for the interest as well.'

* * *

A fellow hired a Kerryman to milk his cows. One morning he found him forcing a cow to drink its own milk from a bucket.

'What the hell are you doing?' he shouted.

'I thought it looked a bit thin,' said the Kerryman, 'so I'm running it through again.'

* * *

How do you recognise a Kerryman in a car-wash?
He's the one sitting on the motor-bike.

* * *

A Kerryman once went to England looking for a job with Weetabix the builder.

* * *

Two Kerrymen were visiting the cinema for the first time. When they arrived the film had already started, so it was quite dark. As they walked down the aisle they were followed by the usherette with a torch.

'Watch out,' said one Kerryman to the other, 'here comes a bicycle.'

* * *

A Kerryman working as a painter on a building site was painting a door at a furious rate. When the foreman asked him to explain he blurted out:

'I'm doing it quickly before the pot of paint runs out.'

* * *

Two Kerrymen went on a holiday to France and stayed at a country farmhouse. They were disgusted to find that everybody in France, even the kids. spoke French. One morning they were awoken by a cock crowing.

'Do you know,' said one Kerryman to the other, 'that's the first word of English we've heard spoken since we arrived.'

* * *

A Kerryman got a job commanding a fire brigade. One night the brigade was called to a small fire. The Kerryman shouted out, 'Hold it a minute and let it burn up a bit so we can see what we're doing.'

* * *

Two Kerrymen were watching a John Wayne film on television. In one scene John Wayne was riding madly towards a cliff.

'I bet you £10 that he falls over the cliff,' said one Kerryman to the other.

'Done,' said the second.

John Wayne rode straight over the cliff.

As the second Kerryman handed over his £10, the first said, 'I feel a bit guilty about this. I've seen the film before.'

'So have I,' said the second Kerryman, 'but I didn't think he'd be fool enough to make the same mistake twice.'

* * *

A tourist in Kerry came upon a level crossing with one gate open and the other gate shut.

'We're half expecting a train,' explained a Kerryman.

* * *

A Glasgow chap visiting Kerry wanted to buy a bicycle costing £200, but had only £120. So he pawned the £120 for £100, sold the pawn ticket to a Kerryman for £100, and bought his bicycle.

* * *

A Kerryman was sick and tired of people heartily slapping him on the back when they met him, so he devised a plan. He put half a dozen sticks of dynamite under his jacket and said, 'There! the next fellow who slaps me on the back will have his stupid arm blown off.'

* * *

A Kerryman got a job as an electrician and his first assignment was to mend a broken door bell for an old lady.

After an hour, he returned to his employer and reported, 'The old lady wasn't in. I rang the bell three or four times, but there was no reply.'

* * *

Two Kerrymen were passing by a nudist colony, so they decided to peep in over the wall and see what was going on inside. So one Kerryman stood on the other's shoulders.

'Are there men and women there?' asked the lower Kerryman.

'I can't tell,' said the upper Kerryman, 'they've got no clothes on.'

* * *

How do you get forty Kerrymen into a Mini?
Tell them it's going to Dublin.

* * *

A Kerryman boasted that he had an axe that had lasted over a hundred years. It had been fitted with only five new heads and eight new handles.

* * *

How do you recognise a bath made in Kerry?
It's got taps at both ends to keep the water level.

* * *

## KERRYMEN HIT BACK

It was only to be expected that Kerrymen wouldn't take all those jokes lying down. Scarcely had the echoes of the last Kerryman joke died away when the counter-attack began. Nobody was spared and the Kerryman as usual had the last laugh.

* * *

What is black and frizzled and hangs from the ceiling?
A Galway electrician.

* * *

What do you call an intelligent Mayoman?
Lucky.

* * *

What is red and white and floats upside down on the Lee?
A Corkman caught telling Kerrymen jokes.

* * *

Why do Tipperarymen always carry a little rubbish in their pockets?
Identification.

* * *

What's the difference between a Clareman and a bucket of fertiliser?
The bucket.

* * *

A Donegalman rushed into a barber's shop with a pig under his arm.

'Where did you get that?' asked the barber.

'I won him in a raffle,' said the pig.

* * *

What is the thinnest book in the world?
The Waterford book of knowledge.

* * *

How do you save a Limerickman from drowning?
You don't know? Good.

* * *

*MORE MERCIER BESTSELLERS*

THE BOOK OF KERRYWOMAN JOKES :
Laura Stack

JOKES FROM THE PUBS OF IRELAND :
James N. Healy.

THE WORST KERRYMAN JOKES :
Des MacHale

OFFICIAL KERRYMAN JOKE BOOK :
Des MacHale

THE BOOK OF KERRYMAN RIDDLES :
Sonnie O'Reilly

IRISH LOVE AND MARRIAGE JOKES :
Des MacHale

THE BOOK OF CORKMAN JOKES :
Des MacHale.

THE BOOK OF IRISH CHILDREN'S JOKES :
Mary Feehan.

THE BOOK OF IRISH SCHOOL JOKES :
Catherine McCurdy.

THE BUMPER BOOK OF KERRYMAN JOKES :
Des MacHale.

BALLADS FROM THE PUBS OF IRELAND :
James N. Healy.

GEMS OF IRISH WISWOM : IRISH PROVERBS AND SAYINGS :
Padraic O'Farrell.

SUPERSTITIONS OF THE IRISH COUNTRY PEOPLE :
Padraic O'Farrell.

THE BOOK OF IRISH CURSES :
Patrick C. Power.

IRISH FAIRY STORIES FOR CHILDREN :
Edmund Leamy.

IRISH FOLK STORIES FOR CHILDREN :
T. Crofton Croker.

IN MY FATHER'S TIME:
Eamon Kelly.

LETTERS OF A SUCCESSFUL T.D. :
John B. Keane.

LETTERS OF A LOVE-HUNGRY FARMER :
John B. Keane.

A HISTORY OF IRISH FAIRIES :
Carolyn White.